CONTEMPORARY ART CURRICULAR INVENTIONS:

PERMISSION SEEDLING ACCUMULATION

Anne, Allie, Hillary, Lauren, Kim, Deb, Mary, Becca, John, Kathleen, Genevieve, Amy, Lynn, Jacob, Jeanine.

Trinity Christian College / October 19, 2019
Initiated and Edited by Jorge Lucero

INTRODUCTION

On October 19, 2019 I was invited by John Bakker and Ryan Thompson to give a lecture and a workshop at Trinity Christian College in Palos Heights, Illinois. I gave a fifty-minute lecture where I addressed the question: *What modes of operation does an artist need to foster within in a teaching practice in order to continue a robust creative practice?* I proposed eleven modes, which I will mention here without elaboration, since the intent of this booklet is not to answer the question I presented in the lecture, but rather to present the work that we did collectively during the workshop.

The modes of operation are:

Collect things; always be *doing* the literature review.

Like things and think about why I/you like them.

Aim to find the pliability of the material at hand and then test its resistance.

Understand relationships as part of a wider (sometimes slower) contemporary creative discourse.

Know that everyone is brimming with expertise.

Demystify the *labor* = *worth* paradigm.

Read and write to think, not just to explain.

Trust accumulation and duration.

Make iteratively and incrementally constantly.

Document everything.

Work in the realms of the invisible, the demateral, and the indeterminate.

After the lecture we moved to the workshop which was intended mostly as a vocabulary/imagination expansion exercise. This exercise is done with a deep and saturated immersion into instances of contemporary art. The exercise that follows contains three parts and is a miniature version of an exercise I do with my undergraduates usually over a period of 8 to 10 weeks. As such what the students at Trinity Christian created here are mostly seedlings. They are not intended to be finished, prescriptive directions on how to do any one thing. The exercise is meant to engender—whether it takes one day or two months—merely seedlings. It really is up to the reader to come back to these pages repeatedly and trying to see if there is anything of worth here. The worth really doesn't come until action is taken by the reader. These seedlings can be turned into large projects, they can be used as everyday prompts, they can be used to think about something and then quickly be abandoned. They are—even—still fulfilling their purpose when they are being ignored. These seedlings thrive on their invisibility and the duration that sometimes causes it. The tree parts found here are:

1. The actual language I use to walk the students through the exercise of collecting contemporary art curricular permissions.

2. Student constructed directives for use in whichever way the reader may see fit. These directives are derived from the student research indicated in the first section.

3. This part—when I work with students for a long time—usually contains planning matrixes where the directive seedlings are taken and organized by mediums and developmental stages from K-12. Since we only had one day to work on this part the students only populated a few of the rows in the matrixes I usually use. What I have done is taken the prompts and thoughts in those rows and turned them into small paragraph seedlings that can be used—again—however the reader deems fit.

Two more things. You'll notice that this booklet doesn't indicate who—of the participants from the Trinity Christian College workshop—authored what. That is intentional. Since these booklets will firstly be given to the students who made them, it is important that when they revisit them next week, next year, or even ten years from now, that the students feel they authored this entire collection of words. Feeling a sense of ownership over this material opens up the probability that things in this booklet will be used freely and loosely. The last thing is that there are pictures included through this publication. These are documents from the workshop but they in no way capture the specialness of the moment and the nuance of what it meant to be alive together in that moment. There are only a few of us, who will carry that with us and that's just the way it is.

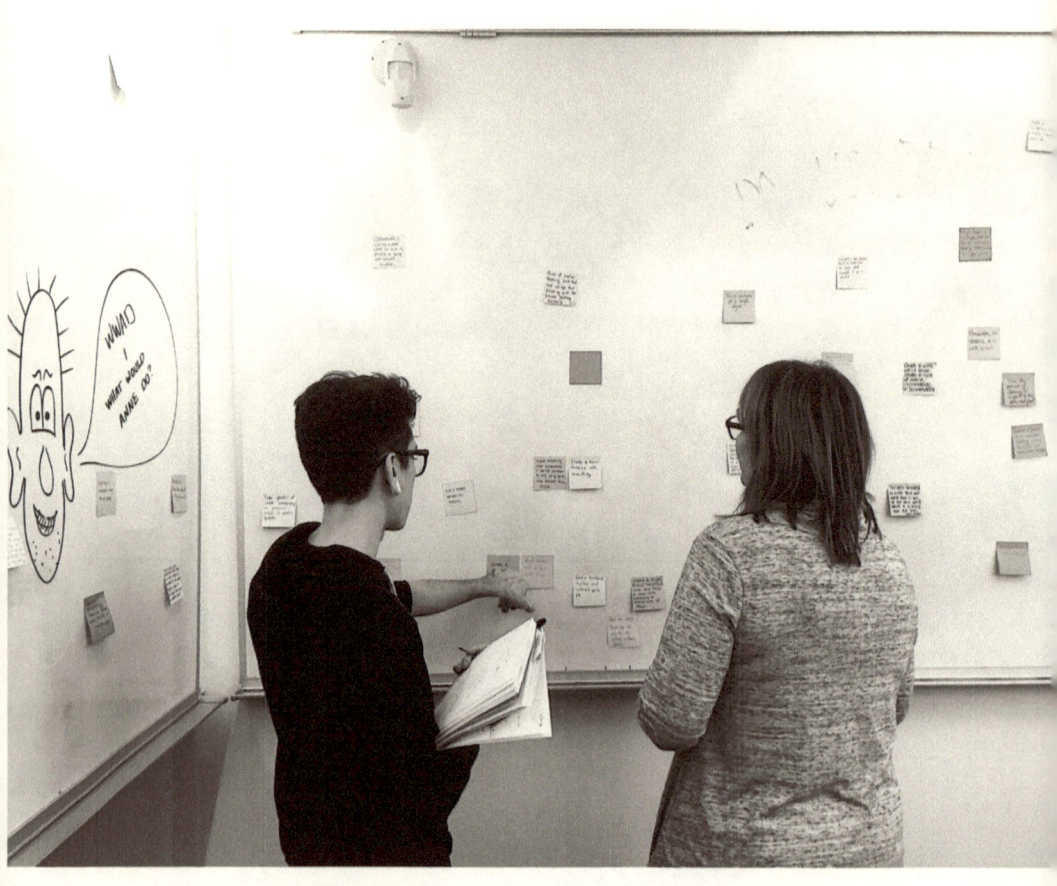

CONTEMPORARY ART CURRICULAR INVENTIONS: PERMISSION SEEDLING ACCUMULATION

For all the years that I have been a college professor I have annually taught an introductory course in art teaching methods. The mode-of-operation_*Contemporary Art Curricular Inventions* aims—not to show students how to write curriculum—but rather to amass an interminable collection of idea seedlings—at the beginning of their teaching practice—for years of art teaching through the languages of contemporary art. These seedlings—in their essence—are the quick product of imaginative contemporary art analysis in order to quickly learn its vocabulary, syntax, and possibilities. This is a search in contemporary art for permissions for our work and the work or our students. Not unlike a scholarly literature review, we look at what has been done before to see what can be done next. It may be where the art teacher goes from being an educational professional to a creative practitioner who just happens to enjoy the challenges and benefits of a professional post.

The *teacher-as-creative-practitioner* is both a cliché and a misunderstood, under-explored phenomenon. On the one hand no one will deny the fact that the teacher is usually asked to think on their feet and to make continuous adjustments both in anticipation of and during the teaching moment. On the other hand, the potential for pedagogical practice to be a contemporary art medium—a new media if you will—is only explored intermittently by artists and teachers, and even less under the long-term commitments of pk-16 schooling. The mode of operation that follows is a challenge for art teachers to experiment with the parameters of what it means to be an artist and what it might mean to be an educator through art. This mode-of-operation aims to open up the invention of curriculum as language-acquisition for art teachers.

Teaching from and into a contemporary art discourses is always an unfinished task; whose vitality is dependent on the same open-ended and generous approach that defines artistic activity. This mode of operation only leads to fragments. The curricular proposals this mode-of-operation produces are purposefully incomplete and they are best presented as such. The motivation for putting incomplete ideas into the world is to invite the readers' creative response to these "open" texts; to open up the possibilities—even for those who author the fragments—to be taught by the incomplete remnants from a very specific gesture of art scholarship.

This mode-of-operation engenders four types of "open" texts: **directives, matrixes** organized around mediums and developmental considerations, "yes-and" **lesson plans**, and iterative **documentation** of attempts to bring the seedlings to fruition.

1. The directive is a direction that is open-ended enough to generate significantly different outcomes from different participants. Directives are made through the scholarly tool that follows this introduction.

2. The matrix is an attempt at organizing some of the directives generated by a participant into media specific and age appropriate lesson-seedlings, or starter ideas, which can be used to initiate curricular thinking. The matrix poses questions intended to focus on the development of future lessons. The focus comes through figuring out and organizing some thoughts on how an artwork can be generated from open-ended directives, what learning actually takes place from these art activities, and how the whole endeavor can be assessed or evaluated.

3. The "yes-and" lesson plan can be seen as the most conventional part of this sequence; however, you are

encouraged to take deliberate care to not make this part the focal point of the process. You will be tempted to firm up this part because it may seem to be the most useful. The truth that the tighter—more prescribed lesson—might help you to complete a very specific lesson, but you may miss out on the opportunity to develop a lesson plan that continues to be fresh every time you revisit it. It is not in anyone's best interest for me to present formulations or prescriptions as to how a given project can be completed; so instead develop lesson plans that serve less as "how-tos" and more like singular possibilities for developing those lesson-seeds into many art-making activities.

4. Finally, if any of these seedlings are to sprout into full blown art activities, over-documentation should occur. Write, photograph, and record everything that happens and that is produced. You never know which piece of documentation will spawn new work in someone who sees it. It may or may not be important to tell the work narrative of the documentation. It all depends on what it is being used for. An image, piece of writing, or recording without context may actually allow the viewer the freedom to imagine the context. Of course, your words can also guide the possibilities. It is a fine line in the end.

MINING CONTEMPORARY ART FOR CURRICULUM THINKING & INVENTING (ALSO KNOWN AS: WHAT PERMISSIONS DO WE GET FROM CONTEMPORARY ART?)

PHILOSOPHY (the thinking behind it)

Unlike any other science, art is one of the only discourses that can be equally participated in by both students and professionals alike. Despite the label of "student", all art-makers are contemporary practitioners and therefore should be engaged as such. This means that it is equally important for a young artist to be exposed to the work of other contemporary artists (their contemporaries) as it is for more seasoned artists. The purpose of this exercise is to quickly generate a diversified collection of contemporary art *languages* that are akin, not only to your sensibilities, but also to the diverse needs of your current and future students. This exercise aims to develop an expanded language for the individual art teacher of what is possible in art **NOW**. The art teacher is, in many ways, a teacher of language invention. For this reason, it is of optimum importance for the art teacher to figure out how to "speak" the multiple languages of art that exist today. As learning a foreign language demonstrates, the most comprehensive way to develop fluency in a new language is via immersion; and so, it is with the language(s) of contemporary art: those who wish to speak the languages of contemporary art, let alone teach from them, must immerse themselves in those languages.

RESEARCH ACTIVITY (what to do)

To begin, find a locale that contains a variety of high-quality examples of art that is being made today. In the best-case scenario a contemporary or modern art museum or gallery is good; in a more everyday scenario, a good art magazine filled with images will do. The art section of your school or town library can also work. Whichever site you're working from make sure that your pool of works is as random as possible, that way you can really explore. Of course, the internet is the ultimate repository of images, but it is mostly uncurated and therefore you may not be coming across works that are part of the current discourse in contemporary art. This is not a legalistic process though, if you have a problem with the implications of only looking at works that have been vetted by a larger community, by all means look and learn from whatever you'd like.

Once you've identified your pool of random works, take a look at them as if you were experiencing them in actuality. Saunter through the museum or gallery, curiously browse at your library or methodically leaf through your magazine. Ask yourself: **1. "How is this *thing* made?"** and **2. "What is this *thing* about?".** These two questions will address the two most frequently occurring concerns in artworks and consequently in art education: form and content. At all times, it is important not to discard your own sensibilities. The works that pull you in or make you inquisitive will find a ready connection to your existing knowledge and experiences and therefore the sharing of the languages in those works with others will be more integral, maybe even genuine. However, don't be hesitant to be challenged by an artwork that doesn't fit neatly within your notions of what art can be. Bringing a challenging art work to a group of students, without first sharing your prejudices about it with them, may reveal an openness to the work on their behalf that will inform *your* reception of it.

Depending on what your site for art is, it may appear very daunting. For example, working from library stacks can be daunting because of the sheer volume of the collection. Going to an encyclopedic museum may also cause you to be overwhelmed. I would suggest that you develop a semi-arbitrary selection process so that you don't spend too much time deliberating your beginning. For example, decide that you will only look at books whose spines are specific colors; or artworks facing a certain direction in the museum. Maybe, you can decide to only select books or artworks of artists' names you cannot pronounce, have never heard of, or are from a certain section in the alphabet, i.e. artists whose names begin with vowels or the letters in your first name. The more complex your selection-device is, the more satisfying your process will be when you begin to see the inevitable (seemingly coincidental) connections emerging between works. These connections might even help you develop themes or connections in your curricular units as well as use divergent artists who "speak" a similar language.

Showing your students variant sources of similar ideas will dissuade your students from thinking that you are saying *any* given project should be done in *any* specific way. Divergent examples that point in the general direction of what you want your students to learn allow for various student interpretations of what you are saying and will consequently produce a plethora of results from your student's thinking and making processes.

In order to make this selection-process work for you, you must assign yourself an overly ambitious goal that you will attempt to meet. The ambitiousness of your goal is necessary so that your eventual failure in meeting that goal will still produce abundant results. For example, determine that you will collect 100 examples in one hour. This of course might be impossible, but your attempt at achieving this goal will produce sufficient results (maybe thirty). When you document your sources, make sure that you include all the necessary reference information so that you could recall that image if needed.

Again, take it slow. Imagine this process like an immersion into *these* worlds of art. It will be in your slow traverse through what is happening in your experience that will allow you to be able to *mine* the richness of the art that exist. We can use the term "mining" since one of our principle roles as art educators is to help dig out the resources that make up our contemporary practice as makers of objects, ideas, and processes in order to grow our imagination about what is possible in art, as well as engage in meaningful conversations about what is being made.

INVENTION ACTIVITY (what's next)

Once you have collected a reasonable amount of contemporary art examples, designate for each work a statement that identifies both elements of its form and content.

You may say something like:

The artist did…,

The artist seems to work in…,

The artist intended to …,

The objective of that work was to…,

When I look at this work it makes me think about…,

I think *(fill in the blank)* is important to the artist.

It is very important that you not attempt to figure out whether your suspicions about the work are true. At this point it is not necessary for you to know whether or not what you perceive to be true, actually is. What is important is **what you think** is happening in the work, since what we are trying to do is develop a set of languages that can then be proposed to our students as directives. From that standpoint it is irrelevant whether or not what you saw or thought you saw was actually what you saw.

After having delineated what your list of works may be about and how they might be made, I would like you to translate those observations about form and content into **specific directives**. Although I want your directives to be specific, I would challenge you to come up with directives that don't specifically describe what you saw in that particular piece of contemporary art. <u>A directive is a direction that is open ended and serves more as a parameter or challenge rather than a method or strictly delineated action</u>. The partial vagueness of a directive allows your students to fill in the gaps and produce work outside of your anticipations.

I will give you an example. Say that you have run across the image of Yoko Ono's "cut piece" (look it up).

You may or may not know that the documentation in those images is of Yoko Ono's Fluxus performance *Cut Piece*. Those facts are only as important as you want them to be for this exercise. You determine that "how this piece was made" **[FORM]** was by:

"the artist uses her body"

or

"the artist uses a collaborator, could be friend could be a stranger"

or

"the artist sits still as something is done to her".

You then determine that "what this work is about" **[CONTENT]** is:

"audience participation"

or

"the objectification of the woman artist/body"

or

"vulnerability".

Whatever you decide is fine; you need not worry about how correct you are in your observations since even your mis-readings will produce results. Now that you have your ideas about what the form and content might be, formulate those observations into two types of directives, one addressing the **form (F)** and the other the **content (C)**.

Your directives (which are intended for someone else to follow) might read like this:

Present a work that takes place on your body somehow **(F).**

Initiate a work that is only finished when someone other than the original author interacts with it **(F).**

Think about a moment when you were vulnerable; without making the memory totally obvious, start your work from that memory **(C).**

Collaborate in making a work that demonstrates an injustice occurring in the world; be poetic in your interaction **(C).**

Any and all of these directives may be used either in tandem or in contrast to each other. Do this for your twenty most intriguing finds and bring all your notes (artwork information, form and content notes, and directives) to the next part of this exercise, the Matrix development (see below).

So, you'll notice that at this point the process requires you to bring all your notes and what you've collected to class. The reason that this works best with a group is because when everyone comes together then you have 400 directives for a group of 20 students. We usually write them on notecards or sticky notes. We then put them all up and this leads to the completion of the next part, which is the Matrix. In the Matrix the seedings get more robust because you stretch the imagination to consider activities, learning, and assessment of that learning. A very important thing I usually do with my students is we don't put our names on any of this work because at the end all the work is given back to the students collated, professionally bound, and ready to be used. You can see an example of one of these books in this BOX FILE.

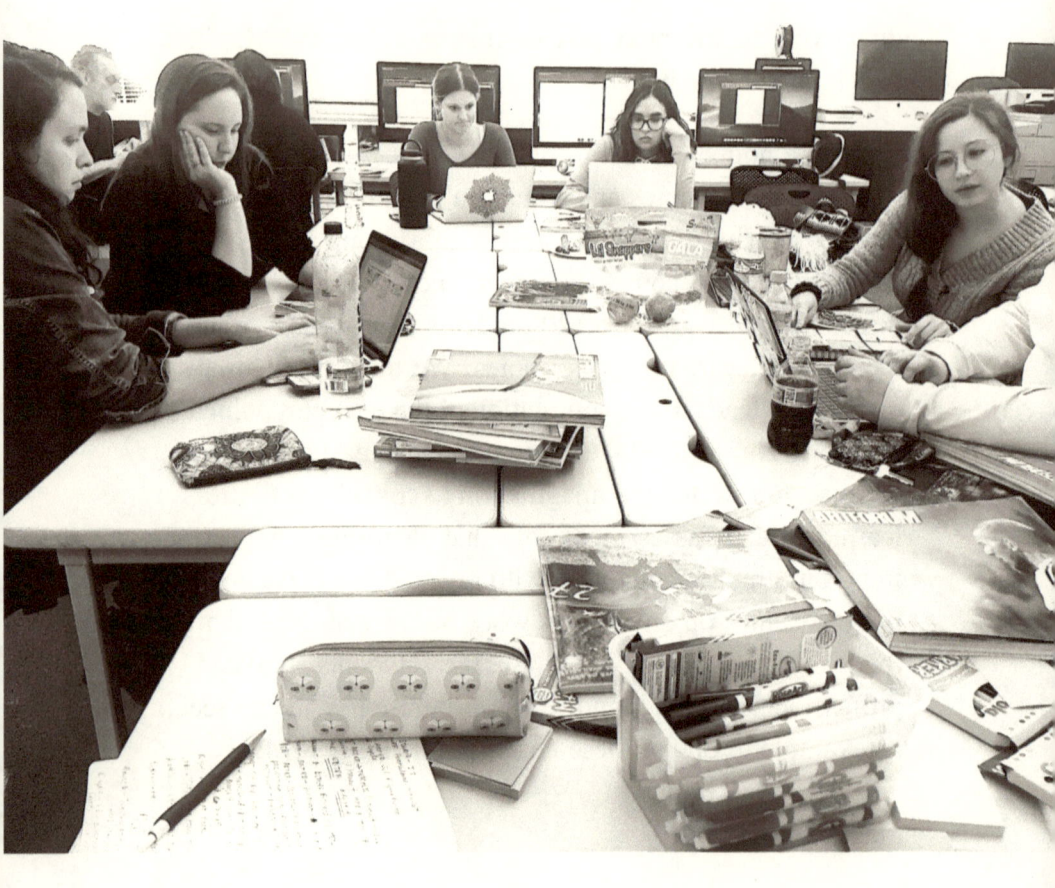

DIRECTIVES

~ Hang a work in which second and third order effects take place.

~ Collect a series of images to present.

~ Present work in which anonymity takes part.

~ Think about the impermanence of human effort and make work from that idea.

~ "Is Identity integral to making art?". Answer this question in your work.

~ Collaborate in making a work about the lack of privacy of living on social media.

~ Create a neon light installation piece.

~ Create a series of color studies about analogous colors.

~ Simplify an object that is familiar to you and repeat as a motif.

~ Demonstrate a type of emotional connection.

~ Photograph a series that talks about idealization.

~ Take photographs of people interacting in unusual ways in public spaces.

~ Make work that rethinks the way we inhabit the spaces around us.

~ Fill a canvas with paint in a way that overwhelms the viewer.

~ Fill a canvas with paint in a way that makes you feel calm.

~ Draw something that makes you uncomfortable.

~ Represent one of your fears in a sculpture.

~ Make a painting that references something you see outside your window.

~ Photograph something that you see every day.

~ Make a drawing that looks like it is 3-D.

~ Say something about your everyday experience.

~ Trick your viewer.

~ Cut up paper media and make work out of it.

~ Paint using pieces of a map.

~ Create work that makes you relive your memories.

~ Search for beauty in the everyday.

~ Photograph portraits of people with their faces hidden.

~ Make an installation that covers an entire wall.

~ Make work that questions reality.

~ Use chalk to make art that does not last.

~ Have people perceive you, invite them to make something that is you.

~ Play with fabric to make it keep forum.

~ What are glossy aspects of people, how do we display that?

~ Take something broken and make it worth something again.

~ Eat an egg. Describe the insides of it for others to understand.

~ Document loss of volition.

~ Mix oil with something. Create. Form.

~ Make a sculpture out of objects found outside.

~ Reinvent a household object. Attempt to use it. Document the outcomes.

~ Where do you see power dynamics in the world? Crave that into something.

~ Document a woman's beliefs.

~ Find a textured surface and interacted with it.

~ Show facts in a nonsensical way.

~ Confuse a viewer, try to make the unknown known.

~ Make something black and white.

~ Find rocks and sculpt with them.

~ Make a fort that blends into nature. Invite people to find it.

~ Do something over the top, document it.

~ What addictions do we have in everyday life, show how we hide those addictions.

~ Take a photo of a pretty person, try and make him unnoticed.

~ Draw something hidden in another thing.

~ Gather copper objects and create with them.

~ Ask a child to describe themselves to you. Get inside their head and create like them.

~ Present a work that includes both photo realism and digital aspects.

~ Think about certain expectations you hold of yourself and others, and consider the unwanted (and sometimes unfair) pressure those expectations might be causing.

~ Consider the absence of a work of art.

~ Initiate a work of art based on identity or lack thereof.

~ Document something beautiful you see every day.

~ Think about your worldview/ideals, start your work based on something you would change about a worldview (your own or someone else's).

~ Start to create a work of art based on something you like.

~ By only using a piece of rope and a pair of scissors, create something that demonstrates vulnerability.

~ Listen to one song that is upbeat. While listening to the song, on a blank piece of paper draw or color what you feel. Then listen to a song that is slower in tempo. Repeat the second step.

~ Go outside. By only using nature, create something that demonstrates diversity.

~ Use your favorite body part to stamp on paper.

~ Dress as your favorite artist.

~ Find a rotting form.

~ Place objects somewhere they do not belong.

~ Cut a pattern in half.

~ Outline a shadow.

~ Give a human animal-like features.

~ Collect images of the same object.

~ Draw a 3D form as 2D.

~ Stamp an ode to yourself.

~ Recreate your favorite self-portrait.

~ Capture beauty in something that scares you.

~ What makes you feel uneasy?

~ Disrupt something that is uniform.

~ Take an outline and dance it into a new form.

~ Unify differences in the same object.

~ Flatten form.

~ Create a piece using the color blue only.

~ Construct a work that have the illusion of being transparent like glass.

~ Form a work that is purely shape, and no representational form.

~ Make a work that is based on nothing you're feeling at this moment.

~ Create a collage to fit within a shape on the floor.

~ Present a work that references and uses the architecture and interior of the area your presenting the work in. site specific collage.

~ Collaborate on a redesign of a space in the building you find is ugly, make it better to you both.

~ Turn a previous piece into an interior space.

~ Create a print only using split complementary colors.

~ Paint over a collage, but do so in sections, masking other layers as you work.

~ Think of a memory, paint the first memory that comes to mind.

~ Think of another memory, paint that exact memory, and collage the content with the previous memory painting.

~ Present a work that is in black and white.

~ Photoshop various historical figures in the same setting, create a fiction.

~ Who makes you feel helpless, create a collage with that figure.

~ Create a photoshop image of political leaders you do not agree with, make them serve you now.

~ Photograph an aspect of nature you find beautiful.

~ Travel somewhere new, take no photographs.

~ Travel somewhere new, write a poem or eulogy to that place.

~ Think of a place that gave you a moment of bliss, find and photograph another place which instills that similar sense of bliss.

~ Create texture without using paint, then paint over those textures.

~ Reference an image of nature, and abstract it using oil paint.

~ Think about a place that evoke some kind of emotion (beauty, or awe or sadness) and paint that feeling from memory.

~ Paint a specific location that evoke an emotion from you, but paint without looking at the actual canvas or surface.

~ Choose a building typically considered dirty and smelly as the setting for an intimate photograph

~ Write a poem about the feelings associated with the forced separation of a young child from his or her parent

~ Depict a picnic in an unusual setting using familiar yet surprising objects

~ Select three of your personal cultural identities and symbolically represent them in a unified way while also suggesting conflict.

~ Create an unusual way to display one of your body parts.

~ demonstrate an action outside of its expected context using two different mediums.

~ Make a painting of a place setting using nontraditional objects.

~ Assemble a still life using items that you find in two different rooms of your home.

~ Take a living object and depict it in three or more converted forms.

~ Build an instillation that incorporates at least three different natural smells that evoke a family tradition, religious experience, or consumer experience.

~ Using line (rope, yarn string, extension cords, ribbon, spaghetti, tape) create an installation that makes people aware of their physical height.

~ Using line fill a space so that that people wish they could enter but can't.

~ Collaborate/collage on an image that seems realistic but creates an ambiguous perspective.

~ Execute circular forms within circular forms.

~ Photograph things that are impossible.

~ Find a process of making and abuse it till you find a visually arresting image.

~ Find the tracks of objects through a space and record them.

~ Lean a vertical object on another vertical object.
Repeat.

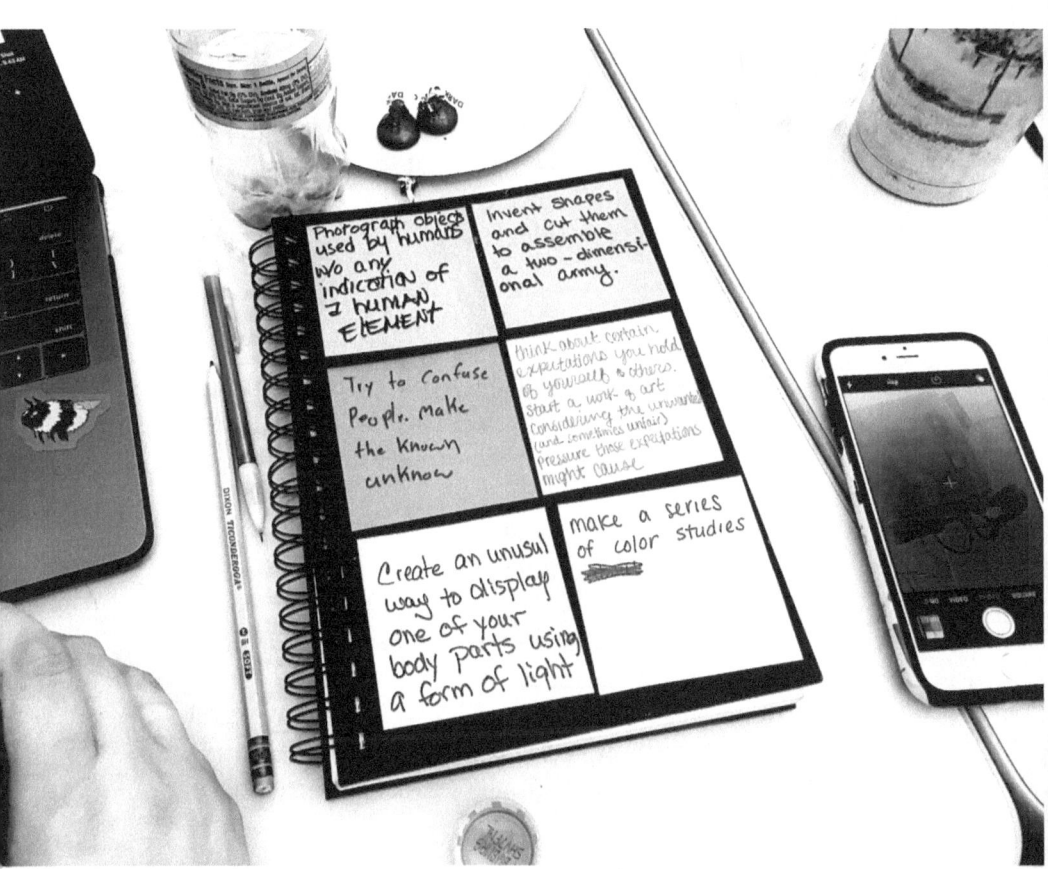

MATRIX SEEDLINGS

A note on this section:
This is the most incomplete of all the parts of this book, but it may prove to be the most fruitful. We are not able to complete these matrixes, but what follows is individual rows on the matrixes that did completed or at least got close. Each one deals with four prompts which are each listed here:

Brainstorm through Directives: (starting from the "wall" of directives: select two directives to work from)

C: What is the work about?
F: How is the work made?

Imagine Activities that might lead to learning: What <u>might</u> the students learn with these directives? What type of skills, craft, or research methods might you show examples of? Exemplars of "modes of operation" (e.g. artists, artworks, etc.)

What new things (learning) can a student expect to come away with: Including new "modes of operation" that the student will be exposed to, what new content will the student be expected to carry into future work? New vocabulary? New ways of fusing disparate knowledge? New content, histories, and critical perspectives?

Evaluation: How will you measure the results for the students and for you? What types of devices can you implement to check for comprehension, synthesis, and potential future use?

———

Each Matrix entry here is accompanied by a suggested grade level.

———

For grade 3
Draw a comic about a time you got in trouble. Explain why you did it and what happened to you in the end. Before the project is introduced read the children "If you give a mouse a cookie" to show a mess that happened and how it was resolved in the end. Ask children to think of a time they actually got in the trouble. They can use markers, crayons or colored pencils. Helps children to be honest about past mistakes even if it makes them feel uncomfortable at first. Helps foster honesty and greater responsibility. Their comic looks at an actual mistake

they made. Creatively shows the sequence of their actions and outcomes. The child is open and honest as they can about their mistake.

****

For grade 5
Find images from print material and make a comic that examines your culture's positive and negative qualities. How do these make you feel empowered or disempowered? Look at Megan Archer work. How she explores detachment and dislocation to self and culture. Also, look at the hungry hungry caterpillar to show that they do not have to seek out figures alone when making a comic on their culture. Allow children to express qualities in their culture they enjoy engaging with and make them feel empowered, but also them to be critical of the circumstances they live in. The children display art that looks at how they live in the world and their culture; both positive things and negative things. They use the collage method creatively and break normal boundaries.

****

For grade 9
Go outside find objects that are either man made or natural, all different however and create structure or sculpture that unifies the objects you've found into a coherent piece. Look at Andy Goldsworthy's work. See how he uses objects found in nature to be interesting and unified sculptures. Invite people to talk about sculptures they've seen or natural or man-made objects that seem to

use diverse materials. Look at how diversity is necessary because it brings more to the table and allows interest to be present in the world. The natural and man-made world can collide in positive ways. Student should be using a variety of different materials and explore ideas of unity within difference. Look at how they and others contribute to society and the world as a whole.

****

For grade K
Recreate a self-portrait. Reinvent a household object and attempt to use it. Ask students how other people might describe them. Applying parts of their identity to objects vocab: represent, symbolism; can't just be favorite things or favorite toys. Find an object around your house that represents you and have them carry it around with them as if it's an accessory. Explain to someone why that object represents you.

****

Recreate a self portrait
Create a work of art based on identity
Rembrandt- the fashions he wore changed with his societal status and success/ Mary Cassatt- painted a specific "type" of person. In art history portraits include fashion items to indicate the subject's class and title in society. Think about what represents you.

Where do you spend most of your time?

Thinking of fashion being the places where you spend your time. Take photos of a favored object or something that represents you and take photos of it in places that you frequent.

****

Recreate a self-portrait.
Reinvent a household object and attempt to use it.

Use unorthodox and unexpected inspiration as material to create garments. Use common household object as inspiration to create a wearable garment and take a photo of yourself wearing it.

****

Do something over the top.
Initiate a work of art based on identity or lack thereof.
Cliché Instagram posts/ Fashion as "distinctive or peculiar/ And often habitual manner or way"

Look at the way social media perpetuates stereotypes. Put together an outfit that shows the irony of an Instagram stereotype or type.

****

For grade K
Photograph objects used by humans without any indication of a human element.
Make a series of color studies.

Kindergarteners will use iPads to find primary colors in man-made objects. Try to take a photo of primary colors without anything in the background.
Students will learn about primary
colors and using the camera app on
their iPads. Students will learn the vocabulary of primary colors.

Students will take pictures of objects compiled into one image to create a monochromatic image.

****

For grade 1
Invent Shapes and cut them to assemble a two-dimensional army. Create an unusual way to display one of your body parts using a form of light. Students cut out shapes that represent body shapes and hold it up to their body while discussing shape. Students will learn to think differently about 3-d objects and turning them into 2-d objects. Talk about shapes that are made. Understand that the body is made up of forms.

****

For grade 2
Recreate a self-portrait.
Give a human animal-like features.
Students will create a found image project of animals that looks like themselves using Bazzart.

Students will learn how to use the app Bazzart to create art. Students will learn about found object art and using a photo app to create brand new art. Students will learn about found image art.

****

For grade 3
Simplify an object that is familiar to you and repeat it as a motif. Collaborate in presenting a mural of colors that convey emotion. Students will create a file in Illustrator of an everyday object and then tile it. Together small groups of students will choose colors to create a giant mural that conveys emotion. Students will learn basic illustrator functions as well as how to tile images. Together students will talk about emotion and what color can convey when it comes to color. Students will understand how to use illustrator basics.

****

For grade 4
Make something hidden in another thing.
Combine multiple layers of organic shapes.
Use Photoshop to make a layered image of organic shapes that create a hidden image. Students will learn to use photoshop to create complex layered images. Learn about how layers can create

****

For grade 1

Collect images of the same object.
Listen to one upbeat song and on a blank piece of paper color or draw what you feel. Now listen to a slower tempo song and repeat the 2nd step. Pick a shape that makes you feel upbeat or happy. (No circle or heart.) Review definition of upbeat and identify emotion and connect emotion and color to a specific image. Finger print to the beat; multiple colors, multiple finger. Connect mood, color, shape and music. Exposure to music and chosen songs. When you feel happy, what color do you think of?

Using different colors for different tempos, tap and print. (Long paper) Anticipatory Set: Play rhythm and "act out" different lines. Can students articulate mood and shape, mood and rhythm? Formative Assessment/Checklist: Are students correctly matching/demonstrating a rhythm?

****

For grade 9
Cut a pattern into pieces.
Document a loss of volition.
Discussion of pattern and repetition; explore examples of wallpaper. Sketch a pattern then add something to it. Repeat but subtract something from it. Draw and print (Styrofoam print) a series of lines inspired by the wallpaper sketches, and print using no more than 1 ink color, but print on multiple colors of paper. Subtractive printing technique. Exchange and cut prints, then collage them together to form a new composition.

How are we cutting them up? (Sol Lewitt, Bridget Riley, Sean Scully, Jasper Johns, quilts). Basic printmaking techniques and steps.

****

For grade K
find beauty everyday
and combine multiple layers of organic shapes.
Leo Leoni kids' books, showing simple forms and colors reflecting the beauty in everyday life through abstracted figures and scenes. "A Color of his own" book
Learning what is beautiful, introduction to simple aesthetics, noticing what interests them, and noticing shapes in abstract ways.

****

For grade 1
Outline a shadow and cut a pattern in pieces. Sergio Gomez art, he traces himself, as we will trace our shadows. Learning to work collaboratively, learning cutting, learning light and shadow, communications, parts and whole relationships,

****

For grade 3
Find rocks and sculpt with them and collect images of the same object. Andy Goldsworthy, sculpts using the natural resources. What is sculpture, appreciation for nature, relating forms to physical features, building/

working with hands, motor skills, Balance and weight, related to Legos, introduction of texture, color, flat versus dimensional, weight

****

For grade 5
Present a work that is in black and white, representing one of your fears/
Guernica by Picasso. Learning to express yourself through marks, lines, and shapes not just color. Reflection of self/ introspective and expressive.

****

For grade 7
Create a modern day still life using two or three normal objects from home using found objects that make you feel uneasy.
Cezanne & Vermeer, old Dutch masters   What a still life is, common everyday objects, and reflecting the beauty of the everyday.

****

For grade 9
Photoshop various historical figures in the same setting, and create a photoshop image of political leaders you do not agree with, make them serve you now. Robert Rauschenberg/ Reexamining history and the problematic side of humanity and politics; having students find either

own agency; examining the students own ethics, finding the students voice in the world (everything is political).

****

For grade 10
Travel somewhere new, write a poem or eulogy to that place; today is today, create what tomorrow is, that is passing time, words to your past self.

John Giorno, Ann Hamilton   Abstract writing and reflection, about time passing, place and self. Symbolic language through artistic writings. Introspective and expressive writing exercise.

****

For grade 11
form a work that is purely shape, no representational form, using two different mediums demonstrate and action outside of its expected context

Rebecca Morris, Wassily Kandinsky, and Richard Serra (Verb List)

Learning abstraction, avoiding using representational figures, formal qualities discovered through experimentation with mediums, color, and material. And exercise in abstraction.

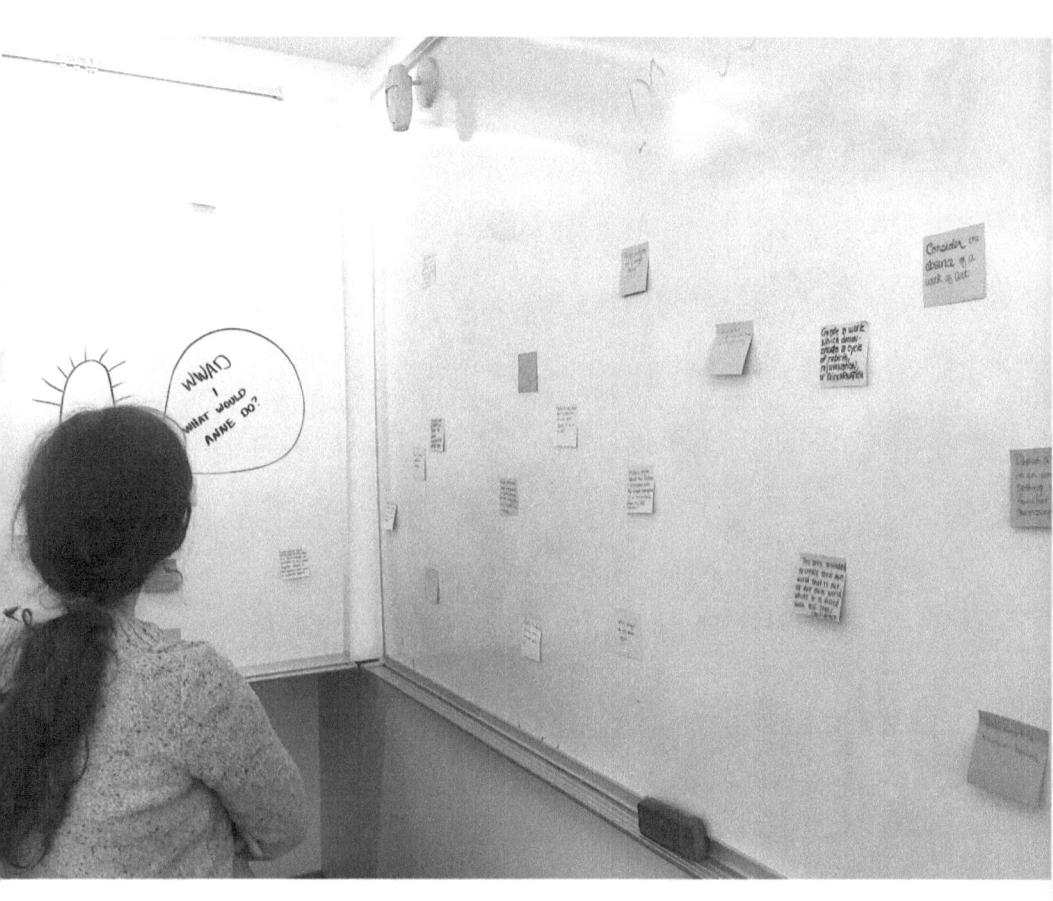

With appreciation to the students of Trinity Christian College, John Bakker, Ryan Thompson, and Jean Carey.

www.ingramcontent.com/pod-product-compliance
Lightning Source LLC
Chambersburg PA
CBHW030736180526
45157CB00008BA/3196